UNIQUE I.M.P.A.C.T.™

STRATEGIES OF SUCCESS FOR AGENTS OF C.H.A.N.G.E.™

DR. SHATOYA BLACK

EDITED BY
NICOLE QUEEN

Vision Publishing House
support@vision-publishinghouse.com
www.vision-publishinghouse.com

ISBN: 978-1-955297-82-0
LCCN: 2025900224

To the trailblazers and change agents— your unique impact transforms lives and builds legacies. May this book inspire you to amplify your voice, embrace your power, and lead with love in action.

"Alone, we can do so little; together, we can do so much."

— HELEN KELLER

CONTENTS

INTRODUCTION

The essence of Unique I.M.P.A.C.T™ (Individuals, Making, Plans and Changing Together) lies in recognizing that we are each uniquely equipped to create meaningful change—not just in our own lives, but in the lives of others and the communities we touch. This concept is about transforming personal trials into collective triumphs, turning lessons into leadership, and reshaping challenges into opportunities. It calls us to celebrate our individuality while embracing the power of collaboration, demonstrating that the greatest impact is made when we act together with purpose and love.

At its heart, Unique I.M.P.A.C.T.™ is a movement rooted in community service, unconditional love, and unity. It asks us to go beyond words and promises to take deliberate action, showing love in ways that uplift and empower those around us. The impact we create is not just about what we accomplish individually, but how we build bridges between people, challenge systems of inequity, and ignite transformation in the spaces we inhabit.

The principles of Unique I.M.P.A.C.T™ encourage a holistic approach to success, blending personal growth with collective empowerment. Success isn't just about reaching individual goals—it's about sharing resources, amplifying voices, and making room for everyone to thrive. Often, people are told they are part of a "community," yet they remain unseen or unsupported. Unique I.M.P.A.C.T.™ challenges this notion by focusing on intentional collaboration, partnership, networking, and experiential experiences to ensure that no one is left behind and that every person's unique perspective is valued and honored.

This journey begins with self-awareness and self-worth. Before you can empower others, you must overcome the barriers that attempt to silence your voice, devalue your experiences, or diminish your confidence. By breaking free from harmful labels and narratives, you step into your God-given identity, recognizing your inherent worth and potential. This foundational shift is not just about personal transformation; it equips you to become a catalyst for change—a person who empowers others to navigate their own growth and empowerment.

Unique I.M.P.A.C.T.™ also emphasizes the importance of acknowledging systemic barriers that affect individuals and communities. Redlining, educational inequities, and the school-to-prison pipeline are just a few examples of the obstacles many face. However, these barriers are not insurmountable. Through awareness, education, and resilience, we can build beyond the structures that perpetuate inequality and create opportunities where none previously existed.

The power of your story is central to Unique I.M.P.A.C.T.™ Your voice, shaped by your lived experiences, is a tool for liberation—not just for yourself, but for others. By speaking authentically and sharing your truth, you not only claim your own narrative, but also inspire those around you to do the same. This is the ripple effect of Unique IMPACT™: when one voice rises, it empowers others to rise, as well.

The legacy of Unique I.M.P.A.C.T.™ is built on three pillars: love, empowerment, and unity. When we serve others with love, we open hearts and create space for healing and change. When we empower individuals, we give them the tools to overcome challenges and realize their potential. When we work in unity, we amplify our collective strength, creating a force for transformation that reaches beyond what any one person could achieve alone.

This is the vision of Unique I.M.P.A.C.T.™: a world where personal growth and collective action come together to build something extraordinary. By embracing your unique role in this journey, you become part of a movement that redefines success, challenges injustice, and creates lasting change. Together, we can leave a legacy of love, empowerment, and impact that will resonate for generations to come.

Let this be your call to action: step into your uniqueness, embrace your role as an agent of C.H.A.N.G.E.™, and make your impact on the world. The journey begins with you, but the transformation will reach far beyond. Together, we are capable of extraordinary things— together, through strategic innovation we make a Unique I.M.P.A.C.T.™

Overcoming Word Curses and Labels

Words hold immense power. They shape our perceptions, influence our actions, and have the potential to either uplift or destroy. Therefore, it's essential to delve into the journey of identifying and overcoming word curses and harmful labels that seek to define us. It's about breaking free from those negative words that are directly or indirectly shaping our perspective to embrace our true identity, and rewrite the narrative of our lives.

The Power of Words

Words have an unmatched ability to create, transform, and empower. They can build bridges, heal wounds, and inspire greatness, lifting us toward our highest potential. Yet, this power comes with a duality: words can also tear down, inflict deep pain, and leave scars that linger long after they are spoken. The power of words lies in their capacity to embed themselves into the fabric of our hearts, spirit, emotions, and minds, shaping not only how we see ourselves, but also how we interact with the world around us. Words can become the lens through which we view our lives, either as a source of hope or as a weight that holds us back.

The Bible reminds us of this profound truth: "Life and death are in the power of the tongue" (Proverbs 18:21). This scripture serves as a call to mindfulness, a reminder of the responsibility we carry in how we speak to others and to ourselves. Words are not fleeting—they carry the potential to either breathe life into someone's dreams or stifle their growth with doubt and fear. Whether spoken intentionally or carelessly, they take root in ways we often fail to realize, shaping destinies with their echoes.

In my own journey, I encountered words that sought to confine and limit me. Phrases like, "You're just a statistic," "You'll never amount to anything," and "You're too difficult" were not just statements—they were weapons. These words were wielded with the intent to diminish my self-worth and potential. And for a time, they succeeded. I allowed those words to settle into my spirit, questioning not only my abilities, but also my value as a person. Their repetition was like a drumbeat, drowning out the truth of who I was and distorting the way I viewed my identity.

The impact of these harmful labels didn't stop at how I saw myself —they also influenced how I moved through the world. I found myself shrinking, questioning whether I belonged, whether I was worthy, whether I could overcome the narratives others had written for me. The words became an invisible barrier, holding me back from opportunities and clouding my ability to dream boldly.

But just as words have the power to harm, they also have the power to heal and restore. Recognizing this truth became the first step in my journey to reclaim my identity and rewrite the narrative of my life. I had to confront those harmful words, denounce their power over me, and replace them with affirming truths about who I was created to be. It wasn't an easy process, but it was a necessary one.

Words matter. They matter deeply. They are not simply sounds or letters—they are carriers of intention, emotion, and influence. Whether used to uplift or to wound, their impact reverberates far beyond the moment they are spoken. That is why it is vital to wield this power responsibly, with love, care, and an awareness of the profound effect our words can have on ourselves and others.

Labels That Bind

Labels, whether intentionally harmful or subtly dismissive, have a way of latching onto us and weighing us down. They can feel like invisible chains, quietly limiting our growth, shaping the opportunities we pursue, and forcing us into boxes that fail to reflect the fullness of who we truly are. The most insidious part is how quickly we internalize these labels, allowing them to shape our self-worth, dictate our choices, and cap the potential we once believed we had.

For me, words like "unlovable," "too much," "too deep," "difficult," "being lied on" or "undeserving" seemed to echo in the hardest moments of my life. They showed up in rejection, reverberated in betrayal, abandonment, and gained power in moments of misunderstanding and lies to my character. They were declarations that began to seep into my spirit, whispering lies about my value and abilities. Over time, they didn't just sting; they started to shape how I viewed myself. I found myself asking: *Am I really unworthy of love? Am I truly too much for anyone to handle?* These labels didn't simply hurt—they began to define me, overshadowing the truth of who I was, pureness of my heart, and the purpose I was called to fulfill, as I navigated barriers.

But as heavy and binding as these labels were, there came a turning point in my journey—a moment when I realized something profoundly liberating: *I am not what they said about me.* I began to see that these words and labels were not reflections of my true identity, but rather lies rooted in others' perceptions, biases, envy, jealousy, insecurities, and fears. They were attempts to box me into a narrative that was easier for others to process, one that often said more about their own limitations than about me. This realization was a breakthrough. It was the first step in reclaiming my narrative and rewriting the story of who I was and who I was becoming.

The power to break free from these labels didn't come from trying to prove others wrong or seeking their validation. It came from understanding that their words didn't define me unless I allowed them to. I had to consciously reject those labels, denounce their influence, and replace them with affirming truths about my worth and potential. Each time I did, I took back a piece of myself, choosing to see my identity through a lens of truth, not through the distortion of others' judgments.

This process wasn't instantaneous, and it wasn't easy. It required courage to confront the lies and the persistence to declare, *I am not what they said about me—I am more based on God's purposed for me not man.* But with each step, I found freedom from the labels that once bound me. I began to embrace the truth of who I was: someone who is worthy, capable, and created for a purpose far greater than others' perceptions. It's the moment I committed to being unapologetically free.

REJECTING THE LABELS

Rejecting harmful labels is far from passive—it is an act of courage, boldness, and defiance. It requires a deliberate, conscious choice to dismantle the narratives that others have imposed on you and those around you. These labels don't simply fall away on their own; breaking free means confronting the words spoken over you, denouncing their power, and actively replacing them with affirming truths that align with who you truly are.

For me, this process was deeply personal and often challenging. I had to face the echoes of words that had settled into my spirit and shaped how I saw myself. When someone called me "not good enough," I didn't just brush it off. I fought back by declaring, "I am more than enough." When others labeled me "a statistic," a phrase meant to diminish my identity and potential, I stood firm and proclaimed, "I am a trailblazer and a legacy leader." Each time I spoke against these lies, I took a step toward reclaiming my power, my identity, and my narrative.

The journey to reject these labels wasn't easy. It required me to unlearn years of ingrained messages—some spoken aloud, others subtly implied. Often, these labels came from people I trusted, including family, friends, and influential figures. Hearing negative labels reinforced by those closest to you can make them feel like undeniable truths. But I learned that rejecting these narratives meant no longer allowing others' perceptions to dictate my reality. I had to realize that their words, no matter how often or loudly repeated, were not the final authority over my life.

Breaking free from these labels demanded that I take ownership of my own story. It required a shift in mindset: understanding that the power to define myself lay in my hands—and in my words. By speaking life and truth over myself, I began to undo the damage of those harmful labels. This wasn't a one-time act, but a daily discipline. Each time I heard the whispers of "not enough" or "undeserving" in my mind, I countered them with affirmations of worth, purpose, and resilience.

Rejecting the labels was not just about denying their validity—it was about rewriting the narrative. It meant stepping out of the shadow of what others had said and embracing a new truth: that I am capable, valuable, and worthy of every good thing. This intentional act of reclaiming my identity didn't just free me from the constraints of others' words—it empowered me to live a life defined by purpose, hope, and possibility.

The Turning Point

There comes a moment in life when you realize you can no longer live under the weight of others' perceptions. For me, that defining moment came when I boldly declared, "I know what they said about me, but they lied." It was a turning point that marked the beginning of my journey to rewrite the narrative of my life. In that moment, I chose to reclaim my identity, no longer willing to let harmful words or limiting labels dictate who I was or who I could become. I did the same for those around me and those whose lives I've impacted, as well.

This shift wasn't just about rejecting the false labels—it was about embracing the truth of who I was and the power I held to redefine my story. I began to see the insidious ways these false narratives had sought to keep me small, boxing me into an identity shaped by others' fears, insecurities, and misunderstandings. They wanted me to believe I was unworthy, incapable, or destined to fail. But I knew better. I recognized that their words were rooted in their limited perspectives, not in the truth of my being. So I stepped out of that box and chose to live authentically, boldly, and unapologetically free. This led to people isolating me, excluding me from invitations, and taking away opportunities. However, I knew that man's "no" could never outweigh God's "yes."

Rewriting my story required courage and intentionality. It isn't about erasing the past; it's about reclaiming it with purpose and power. Rewriting the narrative is about taking every lesson, every struggle, every victory and weaving them into a story of resilience and triumph. This required looking beyond the lies and embracing my unique strengths, my hard-fought resilience, and the rich experiences that had shaped me. It meant celebrating my journey—the trials I had endured, the lessons I had learned, and the victories I had claimed along the way. Each step of my journey declared the power of faith, perseverance, and the belief that I was created for more. My journey is not defined by the labels or word curses others tried to impose on me; instead, it's a story of thriving despite them. I've learned to stop viewing myself through the lens of others' words and instead see myself through the lens of truth—truth rooted in my identity, purpose, and strength.

For so long, labels threatened to define me. When people called me "unprepared," I rewrote the narrative: *I am equipped with knowledge, strength, and strategic innovation.* When they said I didn't belong, I countered with affirmations of truth: *I bring value, wisdom, and a unique perspective to every space I enter.* Rewriting the narrative wasn't just an act of resistance; it was an act of empowerment. I refused to allow someone else's story about me to determine the course of my life.

Although this process involves rejecting negativity; it's more about actively shaping the way you see yourself and the way others see you. It's about flipping the script from victim to victor, from statistic to trailblazer, from misunderstood to deeply rooted in purpose. Rewriting the narrative means embracing the fullness of who you are—the mistakes, the triumphs, and everything in between—and seeing each piece as a declarative statement of your resilience.

When I began to rewrite my story, I no longer felt bound by the labels others used to define me. I affirmed my identity as a woman of purpose, faith, resilience, and an overcomer. I recognized that I was chosen by God—not by chance, but by divine design—to live a life of impact and significance. This revelation transformed how I saw myself and how I navigated the world. I was no longer defined by the opinions of others or the limitations they tried to impose on me. Instead, I stood rooted in the truth of my worth, empowered by the knowledge that I had the ability to shape my destiny. I reclaimed my identity as a woman of vision, influence, and significance. I no longer sought validation from others because I recognized that my worth was intrinsic, not tied to anyone else's perception. The more I owned my narrative, the more I realized the immense power in telling my own story—a story that reflects my faith, my values, and my steadfast commitment to becoming the best version of myself.

Rewriting the narrative is a declaration that you are more than what others have said about you. It's about breaking free from limitations, celebrating your growth, and stepping boldly into the future you are building. It's not about forgetting the past, but reframing it as a foundation for your greatness. This act of reclaiming your story not only transforms the way you see yourself, but also sets an example for others to do the same. By rewriting the narrative, you give yourself permission to thrive in your truth, unapologetically and authentically.

This turning point was not a one-time event, but a daily commitment to choose truth over lies, strength over fear, and purpose over passivity. Each day, I reminded myself that my story was mine to tell and that I had the power to make it one of triumph, hope, and inspiration. This pivotal moment taught me that I am not a product of what was said about me— God is the author of my life, and my narrative is one of resilience, victory, and grace. This marked the beginning of Unique I.M.P.A.C.T.™ (Individuals Making Plans And Changing Together) because I empowered others to join me on this journey and take intentional steps to create meaningful change in their own lives.

Affirming Truths

Affirmations empowered me to break free from the weight of harmful words and labels. They were declarations of truth, designed to realign my perspective with the person I was created to be. I intentionally replaced the negative, limiting words spoken over me with positive, life-affirming truths. Day by day, I spoke over myself: *I am bold. I am strong. I am fearfully and wonderfully made. I am not a statistic. I am chosen. I am a legacy leader.*

These affirmations became my armor. They shielded me from the lies that tried to infiltrate my spirit and sought to remind me of my worth and purpose. Each affirmation was a statement of defiance against the narratives that once sought to confine me. With every word I spoke,

I reclaimed my power and rejected the labels that had no place in my story.

Through this practice, I found healing. Affirmations weren't just about speaking words of encouragement; they were about embracing those words as truth. I surrounded myself with people who spoke life into me, individuals who reminded me of my potential and celebrated my growth. Their words affirmed the beauty and strength I had struggled to see in myself. These relationships were intentional—a support system that affirmed the truth of who I was and who I was becoming. A place where psychological safety was present for me to build trust and growth.

Central to this journey was my connection to God's Word. In Scripture, I found an unshakable foundation of affirming truths. Promises like the following reminded me of my divine worth and purpose:

- "You are fearfully and wonderfully made" (Psalm 139:14)

- "For I know the plans I have for you" (Jeremiah 29:11)

- "I wish above all things that you prosper even as your soul does prosper" (3 John 1:2)

- "Casting down imagination and bringing your thoughts into captivity" (2 Corinthians 10:5)

- "Before I formed you in the womb I knew you, before you were born I set you apart; I appointed you as a prophet to the nations." (Jeremiah 1:5)

- "Write the vision and make it plain on tablets, that he may run who reads it." (Habakkuk 2:2)

- "To give them beauty for ashes, the oil of joy for mourning, the garment of praise for the spirit of heaviness" (Isaiah 61:3)

These verses became anchors, rooting me in a truth that transcended the opinions of others. They reminded me that my identity was not defined by the words or actions of people, but by the love and intention of God, my Creator.

As I continued to speak life over myself, I saw the ripple effects of affirming truths. They not only transformed my own journey, but also empowered me to impact the lives of others. I began to notice how my words could uplift, inspire, empower, liberate, and heal those around me. By modeling the power of affirmations, I encouraged others to reject the false narratives they carried and embrace their own truth.

Affirming truths taught me that healing is an active process—a commitment to replace lies with truth, fear with faith, and doubt with confidence. It is a daily act of reclaiming your voice, your identity, and your power. Through affirmations, I didn't just rewrite the narrative of my life—I created a blueprint of hope for others to follow. This journey showed me that when we speak life over ourselves and others, we contribute to a world where truth, resilience, and purpose reign.

Breaking the Chains

Today, I stand as a living testament to the transformative power of breaking free from word curses and labels. What was once intended to confine me now fuels my purpose. I've shattered the false narratives that sought to limit me, replacing them with a story of resilience, faith, and triumph. My journey is a reflection of what's possible when you refuse to let someone else's words dictate your identity. And I want you to know that you have the power to do the same.

No matter what has been spoken over you—whether words of doubt, dismissal, or judgment—those labels do not define your worth. You are not bound by the misconceptions, expectations, or limitations that others may have tried to place on you. You are not a product of their opinions; they are NOT the author of your story. Allow God to rewrite your story, not as a reflection of their words, but as a declaration of your truth.

Breaking the chains of harmful words and labels is not an easy journey, but it is a liberating one. It starts with acknowledging the impact those words have had and making the intentional choice to release their power over you. It requires courage to confront the lies, strength to replace them with affirming truths, and faith to trust in the greater purpose that lies ahead.

As you take steps to reclaim your narrative, remember that you are not alone. Many have faced similar battles and have emerged stronger on the other side. What makes the difference is the decision to rise above—to see yourself not through the lens of others' words, but through the lens of truth and possibility.

You are not defined by the mistakes you've made, the hardships you've faced, or the labels others have tried to attach to you. You are defined by the strength you've shown, the lessons you've learned, and the purpose you are stepping into. No curse, no label, and no word can take away the truth of who you are.

Breaking the chains is about fully embracing your power, your potential, and your divine identity. It's about standing tall in the face of doubt and declaring, "I am more than what they said. I am everything I was created to be." And with every step you take forward, you are not just breaking free for yourself—you are inspiring others to do the same.

Break free, embrace your true identity, and walk boldly into the life you are called to live. As you move forward, remember that your story is yours to tell. Speak life, reject the lies, and rewrite the narrative. You are more than what they said about you—you are who you are meant to be. And that truth will always prevail!

* * *

Strategy of Success: Rewriting the Narrative

This activity is designed to help you identify and reject harmful words or labels spoken over you, while replacing them with affirming truths that align with your God-given identity and purpose.

1. Identify Harmful Words

- Take a moment to reflect on any word curses or negative labels you have internalized.
- Write down these words or phrases on the left side of a sheet of paper, journal, or in the space below.
- Be honest and specific. For example, "not good enough," "a failure," "unlovable," or "just a statistic."

2. Denounce and Reject

- For each harmful word or label, write a declaration of rejection. Feel free to use the space below.
- Example: "I reject the lie that I am not good enough. That is not who I am or what defines me."

_____

_____

_____

_____

_____

_____

_____

_____

3. Affirm the Truth

- Replace each harmful word or label with an affirming truth that reflects your worth and identity.
  - Examples:
    - Replace "not good enough" with "I am more than enough."
    - Replace "a failure" with "I am resilient and capable of success."
    - Replace "just a statistic" with "I am a trailblazer and legacy builder."

_____

_____

_____

_____

_____

_____

_____

_____

4. Create a Personal Affirmation Statement

- Using the truths you've written, create a personal affirmation statement that reflects your identity. Write it *boldly* in the box below.
- Example: "I am fearfully and wonderfully made. I am bold, resilient, and uniquely equipped to fulfill my purpose."

5. Speak It Aloud Daily

- Commit to speaking your affirmations out loud each day.
- Place them where you can see them—on your mirror, your desk, or your phone—as a constant reminder of who you truly are.

REFLECTION QUESTIONS

- How do these affirmations make you feel when you read them aloud?
- What changes do you notice in your mindset or self-perception over time?
- How can you encourage others to rewrite their narratives and embrace affirming truths?

AGENT OF
C.H.A.N.G.E.

Change is inevitable, but transformation through challenges is intentional. Now, let's step into a space of reclaiming and redefining not just our narrative, but our impact. Let's embrace the change that comes with challenges and step into the role of an agent of C.H.A.N.G.E.™ (Choose to Help Another Navigate Growth and Empowerment)—a catalyst for growth and empowerment, not only in our lives, but also in the lives of others.

THE POWER IN CHALLENGES

Challenges often feel like roadblocks, halting our progress and demanding more from us than we think we can give. But what if we shifted our perspective and saw them not as obstacles to be feared, but as opportunities to grow? The word "challenge" itself holds a hidden truth: embedded within it is the word "change." Every difficulty we face carries the potential for transformation, urging us to adapt, learn, and evolve.

Change, at its essence, is the process of altering, modifying, or replacing something to make it better. But for an agent of C.H.A.N.G.E™, change goes beyond personal development —it becomes a catalyst for waves of transformation that spread outward, influencing others and reshaping communities. Challenges compel us to step out of our comfort zones, confront the unknown, embrace growth, and navigate uncharted territory. And while this may sometimes be overwhelming, it is also where growth takes root.

When challenges shake us, they disrupt our routines and shatter the illusion of control. Yet, these moments of discomfort hold the seeds of our greatest breakthroughs. Challenges are not meant to break us—they are meant to build us. They strip away the superficial and expose the core of who we are, revealing strengths we never knew we had. They teach us resilience, honing our ability to bounce back stronger and wiser. They sharpen our focus, compelling us to prioritize what truly matters. And most importantly, they prepare us for what's next, equipping us with the tools to navigate future trials with confidence.

Change doesn't come from ease—it is forged in the fire of adversity. Every challenge you face is fertile ground for growth, a proving ground for your courage, determination, and faith. It is in these moments of struggle that your capacity expands, your character deepens, and your purpose becomes clearer. Challenges refine you, shaping you into someone capable of creating change not just for yourself, but for others. They remind us that while the path may be difficult, it leads to a destination filled with potential, purpose, and impact.

Becoming an Agent of C.H.A.N.G.E.™

To be an agent of C.H.A.N.G.E.™ is to Choose to Help Another Navigate Growth and Empowerment. Although it has a ring to it, it is more than a title—it's a commitment to a life of purpose, impact, and trans-formation. This role is not just about adapting to change for yourself; it's about taking others by the hand and walking with them through their own journey of growth. Being an agent of C.H.A.N.G.E.™ is a call to action, a deliberate decision to lead, to inspire, and to empower.

The journey of C.H.A.N.G.E.™ requires more than a willingness to adjust to life's shifts. It calls for vision—the ability to see beyond the immediate challenges and recognize the potential within every person and situation. It demands compassion, empathy, respect for lived experiences, and the ability to meet people where they are—offering support and listening without judgment. This empowers individuals to be responsible and accountable for their actions. It calls for intentionality, leadership, courage to step forward, initiative, advocacy, and the ability to guide others toward a brighter, more empowered future.

As an agent of C.H.A.N.G.E.™, you are not a passive observer of transformation and accountability; you are an active participant. You are a catalyst who sparks growth in others, a navigator who helps them find their way, and a source of strength when the journey feels overwhelming. Whether through mentorship, advocacy, teaching, or simply being present, you create spaces where people feel cared for, psychologically safe to grow, challenge themselves, and embrace change.

Your role as an agent of C.H.A.N.G.E.™ extends beyond individual relationships and networking. You become a bridge between what is and what could be, not just for individuals, but for organizations, businesses, programs, teams, communities, and professional development spaces. You help unlock potential by identifying obstacles, providing tools for growth, and creating pathways for success. In doing so, you empower others to step into their purpose, inspiring an effect that transforms and liberates not only their lives, but the lives of those they touch which is L.E.G.A.C.Y.™ unlocked!

The acronym C.H.A.N.G.E.™ serves as a reminder that transformation is not solitary—it is communal. It underscores the importance of choosing to invest in others, helping them navigate the complexities of life while fostering empowerment and self-discovery. By becoming an agent of C.H.A.N.G.E.™, you commit to living with intention, championing growth, bridging the access and opportunity gap, identifying systemic barriers, being a life long learner, and embracing the challenges that lead to lasting change.

The Ripple Effect of Personal Transformation

Transformation is never confined to the individual—it radiates outward, creating a ripple effect that touches countless lives. When you embrace your challenges and allow them to refine and strengthen you, you don't just change your own trajectory—you ignite change in others. Your journey becomes a marker of resilience and hope that inspires those around and and those you encounter to believe in their own potential for growth.

Every step you take toward overcoming adversity sends waves of possibility into the lives of others. You become the living example and trailblazer for your family who will observe your perseverance and gain the courage to tackle their own challenges. Your friends draw strength from your determination, and your colleagues are motivated by your example of authenticity and care. Your transformation becomes a catalyst for change in your community, showing that growth is not only achievable, but also contagious.

By choosing to live authentically and boldly, you give others permission to do the same. You demonstrate that life's difficulties are not endpoints, but stepping stones toward greater potential. The authenticity in your story resonates with others, breaking down barriers of fear, doubt, and limitation. It creates a blueprint for transformation that others can follow, regardless of where they are in their journey.

The ripple effect of personal transformation extends beyond the present moment. It creates a legacy—a lasting imprint on the lives of those you touch. When you lead with authenticity, courage, and compassion, you plant seeds of empowerment that can grow across generations. Families are strengthened, communities are uplifted, and the impact of your transformation and change continues to expand in ways you may never fully see.

Ultimately, your transformation becomes a source of collective empowerment. As you grow, you naturally empower others to embrace their challenges, rewrite their narratives, and step into their own potential. This is the essence of being an agent of C.H.A.N.G.E.™—not only transforming yourself, but inspiring and enabling others to transform their lives, as well.

Breaking Down the Barriers to Change

Being an agent of C.H.A.N.G.E.™ means stepping into the difficult, but necessary work of identifying and dismantling the barriers that stand in the way of progress. These barriers can take many forms—systemic injustices, emotional wounds, societal biases, or even deeply rooted personal beliefs. Challenges have a way of exposing the gaps that need attention, shining a light on the areas where change is most needed.

It is your responsibility as a change agent to not only recognize these barriers, but to work actively to overcome them.

Addressing systemic barriers often means advocating for policies and practices that promote equity, fairness, and inclusion. It requires questioning the status quo and challenging outdated systems that perpetuate harm or stagnation. As an agent of C.H.A.N.G.E.™, you serve as a bridge between what exists and what could be, finding innovative solutions and championing new approaches that bring about meaningful transformation.

On a personal level, breaking barriers involves confronting limiting beliefs and narratives that hold you back. These internal obstacles—self-doubt, fear of failure, or the lingering effects of past experiences—can be just as impactful as external systems. Overcoming them demands introspection, resilience, and a commitment to personal growth. By facing these challenges head-on, you not only empower yourself, but also model what is possible for others.

Dismantling societal biases and stereotypes adds another layer to this work. As an agent of C.H.A.N.G.E.™, you must confront prejudice and ignorance with empathy, education, and a clear shared vision for inclusivity. This isn't easy, as resistance to change is often deeply ingrained. Yet, it is through these efforts that you can create environments where everyone has the opportunity to thrive in the spaces you occupy.

This work is not for the faint of heart. It requires courage to speak out, persistence to keep going when resistance arises, and the ability to stay focused on your vision even in the face of retaliation. It's easy to become discouraged when change feels slow or when opposition feels overwhelming, but focus on the people and purpose. But it is precisely in these moments that your role as an agent of C.H.A.N.G.E.™ becomes most vital.

By breaking down barriers, you are not just transforming the lives of individuals by being responsible for actions of the role you play. As an agent of change you are reshaping the structures and systems that impact them. This work creates a ripple effect, empowering others to overcome their own challenges and contribute to a collective movement of progress. As an agent of C.H.A.N.G.E.™, you are at the forefront of this movement, bridging gaps, building connections, and paving the way for a better, more equitable future.

EMBRACING RESILIENCE

Resilience is the bedrock upon which personal growth and success are built. Every challenge you face, whether it is a minor inconvenience or a life-altering circumstance, adds another layer to your resilience. Resilience goes beyond the ability to recover from setbacks; it is the strength to bounce forward, taking the lessons learned and using them to fuel progress and transformation. Resilience transforms challenges from mere obstacles into stepping stones toward your fullest potential.

Resilience is cultivated through experience. With each challenge you overcome, you gain not only the confidence to face the next, but also the tools and insights to navigate it more effectively. This cumulative growth becomes your foundation, fortifying you against future adversity. Instead of fearing difficulties, you begin to see them as opportunities to refine your skills, expand your perspective, and deepen your understanding of yourself and the world around you.

What makes resilience so powerful is its dual nature—it equips you to handle the unexpected while also serving as a reminder of your capacity for strength. Each time you rise after a fall, you affirm your ability to endure, adapt, and thrive. Resilience becomes a self-reinforcing cycle: the more you persevere, the more resilient you become, and the more resilient you become, the greater your capacity to persevere.

Resilience is not just about enduring hardship; it's about using those experiences to propel yourself to new heights. When you bounce forward, you are not merely returning to the place you were before the challenge—you are stepping into a new version of yourself, one that is stronger, wiser, and more prepared for what lies ahead. It's a reminder that adversity does not define your character; your response to it does.

This foundation of resilience also allows you to approach future challenges with a sense of purpose and perspective. You come to understand that each difficulty carries within it the seeds of growth and opportunity. By viewing challenges through this lens, you shift from a mindset of survival to one of empowerment and progress. You realize that every storm you weather adds to the strength of your foundation, making you unshakable in the face of whatever comes next.

With resilience, even in your darkest moments, you are equipped to handle whatever life throws your way. It is the foundation that supports not only your journey, but also your ability to inspire and uplift others. Resilience is your proof that, no matter the challenge, you have the strength to rise again—and to rise higher than before.

Revealing Purpose and Potential

Challenges are often the most profound teachers, stripping away distractions and forcing you to confront the core of who you are. They bring you face-to-face with your strengths, your vulnerabilities, and the untapped potential that lies within you. In moments of struggle, you are compelled to dig deep, to draw on reserves of resilience, courage, and creativity that you may not have realized you possessed. It is through these trials that your purpose and potential begin to emerge with greater clarity.

When life is easy, it's tempting to stay in the comfort zone, relying on what's familiar and safe. But challenges disrupt that complacency. They require you to problem-solve, to innovate, and to persevere in ways that stretch your abilities. As you navigate these difficulties, you begin to see patterns—areas where you naturally excel, passions that ignite your spirit, and values that guide your decisions. These insights become markers on the path to understanding your purpose.

Purpose is often revealed in how you respond to adversity. What drives you to keep going? What motivates you to overcome? The answers to these questions illuminate the deeper "why" behind your actions, the calling that pushes you forward even when the odds are stacked against you. Challenges refine your focus, helping you differen-tiate between what truly matters and what is merely noise. They reveal the impact you are meant to have on the world, the unique way you are equipped to make a difference.

In this refining process, your potential is also unlocked. The strengths you uncover during tough times become tools for future success. You learn to trust your intuition, harness your creativity, and believe in your ability to persevere. What once seemed impossible becomes achievable, and the limits you placed on yourself begin to dissolve. You start to see yourself not as a person defined by circumstances, but as someone capable of rising and building beyond barriers.

Each challenge you overcome adds to your confidence and expands your vision of what is possible. You begin to understand that your potential is not fixed—it grows with every obstacle you face and every lesson you learn. What you once considered weaknesses become areas of growth, and what you once saw as insurmountable becomes a stepping stone.

Revealing purpose and potential is not a one-time event; it is an ongoing journey. With each new challenge, you gain more clarity and confidence. You come to see challenges not as barriers, but as invitations to step more fully into who you are meant to be. Your purpose becomes a guide, and your potential becomes the fuel that propels you toward a life of meaning, impact, and fulfillment.

TURNING CHALLENGES INTO OPPORTUNITIES

To be an agent of C.H.A.N.G.E.™ allows you to step into the role of a visionary leader, someone who sees beyond the immediate obstacles and focuses on the vast possibilities that lie ahead. Visionary leaders possess the unique ability to navigate challenges with purpose, viewing them not as setbacks, but as opportunities to innovate, grow, and inspire. They are driven by a clarity of vision that transcends circumstances and fuels their determination to create meaningful change.

A visionary leader doesn't just react to challenges—they embrace them, using adversity as a platform for innovation. They approach each obstacle with resilience and creativity, finding solutions where others see roadblocks. Their innovation and adaptability set the tone for those around them, fostering a culture of growth, collaboration, and optimism.

What sets visionary leaders apart is their ability to inspire others. They lead by example, not simply instructing, but embodying the values and principles they advocate. By sharing their struggles and triumphs, they create a powerful narrative that resonates with others, showing them that challenges are not the end, but a new beginning. These stories become sources of hope, reminding others that they, too, have the strength and potential to overcome.

Visionary leadership also requires a commitment to action. It's not enough to dream of a better future; visionary leaders take tangible steps to bring that vision to life. They mobilize teams, build bridges between diverse perspectives, and guide individuals and organizations toward shared goals. Their enthusiasm and determination are contagious, empowering others to step into their roles as change-makers.

As a visionary leader, your story becomes your most powerful tool. By openly sharing your journey—your hardships, breakthroughs, and lessons learned—you give others permission to confront their own challenges with courage and purpose. Your authenticity creates trust and connection, fostering a sense of unity among those you lead.

Moving Forward as an Agent of C.H.A.N.G.E™

Being an agent of C.H.A.N.G.E.™ is a call to action, a commitment to transform not only your own life, but also the lives of those around you. It's about taking the lessons learned from your challenges and using them to light the path for others. It's about fostering hope, standing as a source of strength, and being a catalyst for empowerment. You are the proof that growth is possible and that adversity can be the foundation for greatness.

As an agent of C.H.A.N.G.E.™, your story is a legacy in the making. Every time you help someone navigate their own growth and empowerment, you create a lasting change that extends far beyond the moment. Your encouragement can inspire someone to take their first step. Your strength can give someone the courage to face their fears. Your voice can remind someone that they are not alone. This is the essence of being an agent of C.H.A.N.G.E.™: using your journey to uplift others and pave the way for lasting transformation.

The challenges you face are not a period in your story—they are the beginning of an entirely new chapter. They are the moments that refine your character, test your faith, and prepare you for a greater purpose. These challenges are your training ground, equipping you with the resilience, wisdom, and determination to not only overcome, but to lead others through their own trials to triumph. By embracing these challenges, you transform them into opportunities—for growth, for impact, and for change.

Your journey as an agent of C.H.A.N.G.E.™ carries immense responsibility, but it also holds limitless potential. You might be the first to break a cycle, to forge a new path, or to redefine what is possible, but you won't be the last. Your courage and commitment set the stage for others to follow, proving that transformation is not just for the privileged few, but for anyone willing to embrace the change within the challenge.

As you move forward, remember the effects of your actions. You are a trailblazer, breaking barriers and redefining possibilities. You are a cycle breaker, dismantling generational patterns and building a new legacy. And you are a visionary leader, inspiring others to see beyond their present circumstances and step boldly into their potential.

The change is in the challenge—and it starts with you. You have the opportunity to take the lessons from your journey and use them to make a difference. So, let's begin this journey of transformation together. Let's choose growth, choose empowerment, and choose to leave a legacy that continues to inspire. Your story is far from over, and your impact is only beginning.

* * *

STRATEGY OF SUCCESS: AGENT OF C.H.A.N.G.E.™

This activity helps you embrace challenges as opportunities for personal growth while equipping you to inspire and empower others. By reflecting on the C.H.A.N.G.E.™ acronym (Choosing to Help Another Navigate Growth and Empowerment), you will identify actionable steps to create positive transformation in your life and community.

1. Reframe a Challenge

- Think of a recent challenge you've faced that initially seemed overwhelming.
- Write down the details of this challenge, including how it made you feel and the barriers you encountered in the box below.
- Now, reframe the challenge as an opportunity for growth. For example:
  - Challenge: "I failed at achieving a major goal."
  - Reframed: "I learned resilience and how to approach my goals differently."

2. Define Your Role as an Agent of C.H.A.N.G.E.™

- Reflect on how you can help others navigate growth and empowerment through this challenge.
- Write down one way you can take your personal experience and use it to uplift someone else in the box below.
  - Example: If you overcame financial hardship, you could mentor someone struggling with budgeting.

3. Set Intentional Goals

Write one specific goal for how you will use your role as an Agent of C.H.A.N.G.E.™ in your personal life, workplace, or community. Use the acronym (below) to guide your goal:

- **C**: Choose a specific area to focus on (e.g., education, mentorship, advocacy).
- **H**: Help someone by offering your skills or resources.
- **A**: Actively engage with those who need support.
- **N**: Navigate the process of growth with patience and persistence.
- **G**: Guide others toward achievable outcomes.

- **E**: Empower them with tools, encouragement, and affirmation.

4. Write Your C.H.A.N.G.E.™ Vision Statement

- Create a short statement that captures your purpose as an agent of C.H.A.N.G.E.™
  - Example: "I am committed to turning challenges into opportunities by helping others embrace growth and empowerment through mentorship and advocacy."

5. Take Action Today

- Write down one small action you can take today to start living out your role as an agent of C.H.A.N.G.E.™
    - Example: "I will reach out to someone I know who is struggling and offer my support."

Reflection Questions

- What did you learn from reframing your challenges?
- How does embracing your role as an Agent of C.H.A.N.G.E.™ impact your view of leadership and service?
- Who can you impact today by sharing your story or offering guidance?

_____
_____
_____
_____
_____
_____
_____
_____
_____
_____
_____
_____
_____
_____
_____
_____
_____
_____
_____
_____
_____
_____
_____
_____
_____
_____
_____
_____
_____

BECOMING MORE THAN ENOUGH

There was a time when I felt crushed beneath the weight of expectations, insecurities, and comparison. I measured myself against others based on societal standards and always came up short—at least in my own mind. My inner dialogue was filled with doubt, fueled by the whispers of voices, both internal and external, that seemed to echo the same refrain: You're not smart enough. You're not strong enough. You're not worthy enough. You're not scholarly enough. You are not professional enough. You do not code switch so it's not enough.Your writing is not enough. These lies wrapped themselves around my spirit, making it difficult to see the truth of who I really was.

EMBRACING YOUR GOD-GIVEN IDENTITY

There came a pivotal moment when I could no longer bear the false narratives I had allowed to shape my identity. It was as though a light pierced through the darkness, revealing a truth I had long overlooked: My worth was never something to be debated, negotiated, or defined by others. My identity was already established—rooted in God's truth, not the shifting opinions of the world or the lies of self-doubt.

This realization didn't come easily. It required me to confront the lies I had internalized and actively replace them with affirming truths. I began to ground myself in the promises found in scripture, promises that spoke directly to my heart and identity: "I am fearfully and wonderfully made." "I am chosen." "I am more than enough." "I am equipped and empowered for my purpose." These affirmations were declarations of freedom that reminded me of who God had always said I was.

Faith became my anchor during this transformation. Through prayer, reflection, and moments of vulnerability with God, I learned to see myself through His eyes. I was no longer the sum of my perceived shortcomings; I was a masterpiece in progress, intentionally crafted with a unique purpose. God's truth affirmed that my life wasn't defined by my mistakes, my failures, or the opinions of others. It was defined by His promises, His grace, and His unwavering love.

Stepping into this truth wasn't a one-time event; it was a process. Each day, I had to choose to believe what God said about me to silence the lies the world whispered. It meant intentionally rejecting the narratives that sought to diminish me and embracing the identity that God had already declared. This journey required unlearning years of internalized doubt and allowing God's truth to take root in my heart, mind, and soul.

As I embraced my God-given identity, I found not only freedom, but also a sense of peace and purpose. I realized that I didn't need to be perfect to be impactful. I didn't need to measure up to someone else's standards to be valuable. I didn't need the approval of others to walk confidently in my calling.

This transformation didn't just change how I saw myself—it changed how I moved through the world. I no longer lived in fear of inadequacy or rejection. Instead, I stepped into spaces with the assurance that I was chosen, empowered, and equipped for every opportunity God placed before me. Embracing my God-given identity allowed me to live boldly, authentically, and with purpose, knowing that I am, and always have been, enough. *And so are you!*

FROM INSECURITY TO PERSEVERANCE

The journey from insecurity to perseverance was not a straight path, but a winding one, marked by moments of doubt, struggle, and growth. As

I began to embrace my God-given identity, I started to see how faith and resilience had been quietly shaping me all along. Every challenge I had faced, every setback I had endured, was not a reflection of my shortcomings, but a testament to the strength God had already placed within me.

For years, I had wrestled with the need to prove my worth—to others and, perhaps most of all, to myself. I sought validation in achievements, accolades, and the approval of those around me. Yet, no matter how hard I worked, the sense of being "enough" always seemed just out of reach. It wasn't until I turned inward and upward—seeking God's truth rather than the world's approval—that I realized my worth had never been up for debate. It was intrinsic, established by the One who created me.

Faith became my anchor in this realization. Whenever doubt threatened to pull me under, I clung to God's promises: "I will never leave you nor forsake you." "You are fearfully and wonderfully made." "My grace is sufficient for you." These words became lifelines, reminding me that I was not alone in my journey and that God had already equipped me for the work He had called me to do.

Perseverance became the muscle I strengthened with each trial I faced. Every time I stumbled, I learned how to stand again, a little stronger and a little wiser. I came to understand that resilience wasn't about pretending everything was okay or avoiding struggle; it was about moving forward despite the difficulty. It was about leaning into the lessons that challenges offered and allowing them to refine me rather than define me.

In this process, I discovered that I didn't need to be perfect to make an impact. My flaws, my imperfections, and even my failures were not barriers to my purpose—they were simply part of the journey. They taught me humility, compassion, and the value of perseverance. They reminded me that my journey wasn't about achieving perfection, but about embracing progress and operating in a standard of excellence to excel.

With each step forward, my confidence grew—not because I had suddenly become flawless, but because I understood that my worth was not tied to my performance. I was enough because God said I was enough. I was chosen, called, and capable, not in spite of my imperfections, but because of how God was using them to shape me in my purpose.

The transition from insecurity to perseverance wasn't just about overcoming challenges; it was about recognizing that the strength I needed had been within me all along. My faith unlocked it, and my resilience carried it forward. Today, I stand in that truth, knowing that I don't need to prove myself to anyone . Instead, I simply need to walk boldly in the purpose God has set before me, trusting that He has already given me everything I need to succeed.

Overcoming Impostor Syndrome

One of the most persistent battles I faced was the temptation to give in to social norms– measuring my life against others. In a world that constantly showcases success in carefully curated snapshots, it was all too easy to feel like I wasn't enough—like I wasn't accomplishing enough, earning enough, or simply being enough. Social media feeds, professional milestones of colleagues, and even the well-meaning advice of friends often served as a magnifying glass, amplifying my insecurities. It wasn't just the feeling of inadequacy that weighed me down; it was the relentless pressure to "catch up," to move at someone else's pace, and to prove that I belonged in spaces I sometimes doubted I deserved to occupy because of how I was treated.

Adding to this was the struggle with impostor syndrome—the insidious belief that no matter how much I achieved, it was all a fluke. I feared being "found out," as though someone would pull back the curtain and reveal that I wasn't qualified, that I had somehow stumbled into success by accident. Despite evidence of my hard work and capabil-ity, this inner voice constantly whispered that I didn't truly belong. This was the system of oppression I faced—enduring microaggressions, bullying, and false accusations intended to silence me. I was overlooked for opportunities because of my boldness, subjected to discrimination, and perceived as a threat rather than an asset. People told me, "It doesn't take all of that," or accused me of "doing too much," when in reality, they were not doing enough.

But here's what I've learned: comparison is the thief of joy, and impostor syndrome is a liar. The reality is that my journey was never meant to mirror anyone else's. God's plan for my life was unique to me —crafted with care, purpose, and intentionality. The truth was that I didn't need to compete with anyone to prove my worth. My value wasn't tied to the speed at which I reached milestones or the number of accolades I accumulated although it was evident. It was intrinsic, given to me by God and affirmed by the work I was doing in the world.

The more I focused on my path, the more I realized that each small step forward was significant. The comparison trap had kept me from recognizing the beauty of my own journey—one that was filled with victories both small and large, lessons learned, and moments of grace.

Overcoming impostor syndrome required an intentional shift in perspective. I began to remind myself that I wasn't in any room by accident. Every opportunity, every role, and every success was a result of my preparation, hard work, impact, being an agent of C.H.A.N.G.E.™, and my faith. I embraced the truth that God doesn't make mistakes. If He opened a door for me, it was because He had equipped me to walk through it. I began to affirm and embrace my calling with the mindset of: *I am here for a reason. I am capable. I am enough.*

As I silenced the external voices around me, I stepped into unapologetic freedom. I released the pursuit of what others defined as perfection and instead embraced a standard of excellence that allowed me to thrive. Each step forward, no matter how small, became a testament to my growth. My worth was no longer tied to external validation; instead, I began to recognize and celebrate the progress and growth within myself.

It wasn't that I was ignoring the achievements of others; it was simply that I had learned to celebrate them without dimming my own light. It was about embracing the unique timing and purpose of my journey and trusting that I was exactly where I needed to be. By focusing on my own path, I discovered that the race wasn't about finishing first or following someone else's map—it was about staying true to the one God had set before me. And that path, with all its twists and turns, was more than enough.

EXCELLENCE, NOT PERFECTION

Perfection is a cruel illusion—a moving target that whispers, "If you're not flawless, you're not worthy." It keeps us stuck, trapped in the belief that anything less than perfect is failure. But here's the truth: growth isn't sequential or polished. It's messy, imperfect, and profoundly human. Real progress isn't about achieving a flawless outcome—it's about taking one small step forward, even when the path is uncertain.

For much of my life, I believed the lie that mistakes diminished my value. But over time, I learned that mistakes don't define us—they refine us. They are opportunities to grow, to learn, and to build now for the future. Each stumble on my journey moved me toward self-discovery, strength, and courage.

This wasn't an easy lesson to learn. It required me to shift my perspective and extend grace to myself. Grace to make mistakes. Grace to fall short of my own expectations. Grace to see failure not as the end, but as a new beginning. I had to remind myself that *perfection* was what others saw it as, but excellence was the goal.

Embracing this mindset changed everything. I began to celebrate the small victories along the way. I let go of the need to have all the answers or to get everything "right" the first time. Instead, I chose to see growth as a journey, not a destination. Each imperfect step became a testament to my perseverance, my courage, and my commitment to becoming.

Acknowledging my humanity allowed me to remain unapologetically free. I began to see my flaws not as weaknesses, but as parts of my story that made me stronger. I embraced my strengths without diminishing my worth by what I hadn't yet accomplished. I learned to rest in the truth that I was enough, even in the process of becoming.

This shift didn't mean I stopped striving for excellence, but it did mean I let go of the need to prove my worth. It meant recognizing that the beauty of growth lies in its imperfection. It's in the messy moments of trying, failing, and trying again that we discover our true potential.

Progress, not perfection, became my focus. It reminded me that each day was an opportunity to move forward, no matter how small the step. It encouraged me to focus on the journey rather than the destination and to celebrate the strength it takes to simply keep going.

As I embraced progress, I found a deeper sense of purpose, peace, and holistic wellness. I understood that I didn't need to be perfect to make an impact—I just needed to show up, learn, and keep growing. And in doing so, I discovered a version of myself that was authentic, resilient, and beautifully whole.

You Are More Than Enough

Becoming "more than enough" doesn't mean you've figured it all out or reached some idealized version of yourself. It doesn't mean that insecurities or doubts will suddenly disappear. What it does mean is embracing the truth that your worth was never in question—you've always been enough, just as you are.

This realization is about being authentic and unapologetically free. It's about understanding that your value isn't dependent on your accomplishments, titles, or the opinions of others. Your worth is rooted in something far deeper—in your identity as someone created with purpose, intention, and unique gifts. It's knowing that every challenge you face and every triumph you achieve are shaping you for something greater.

For me, becoming more than enough meant stepping into my God-given identity with boldness. It required letting go of the lies of comparison and impostor syndrome that tried to diminish my confidence. It meant trusting that I was already equipped for the journey ahead, even if I couldn't see the entire pathway to success. Excellence and integrity became my guide, resilience my strength, and faith my foundation. Each step forward was a declaration that I was not only enough, but that I was more than ready to fulfill my purpose.

As you move forward, remember that your journey is not just for you. Your courage to embrace your worth encourages others to see their own. Your resilience in the face of challenges empowers those who are struggling. When you walk confidently in your purpose, you inspire others to do the same. You become a reflection of what's possible, a reminder to those around you that they, too, can overcome challenges and embrace their worth.

So take the first step today. Stand in front of a mirror, look yourself in the eye, and affirm this truth: "I am more than enough." Let these words shape how you see yourself, how you navigate the challenges ahead, and how you impact the world around you. You don't need to strive for worthiness—it's already yours.

Trust in the process. Embrace the journey. Walk boldly in your purpose. And always remember: You are enough, and with every step forward, you are becoming even more. This is your time to shine, to grow, and to leave a legacy that inspires others to do the same. You are now an agent of C.H.A.N.G.E.™ if you will make a pledge to commit to the journey.

* * *

STRATEGY OF SUCCESS: PROGRESS OVER PERFECTION

This activity helps you embrace your inherent self-worth, move past impostor syndrome, and celebrate progress rather than striving for unat-tainable perfection. Through reflection and actionable steps, you will develop confidence in your God-given identity and recognize that you are more than enough.

1. **Identify Limiting Labels and Replace Them with Truths**

- Write down three labels, criticisms, or negative beliefs you have internalized about yourself.
- Next to each one, write a truth that directly challenges and replaces that belief.
    - Example:
        - Limiting Label: "I'm not good enough."
        - Truth: "I am fearfully and wonderfully made, equipped with everything I need to succeed."

2. Celebrate Your Progress

- Make a list of five milestones, big or small, that reflect how far you've come in your journey.
  - Example:
    - "I finished a project despite feeling unsure of myself."
    - "I asked for help when I needed it, which shows courage and growth."
    - Reflect on how these milestones demonstrate your progress and resilience.

3. Create Your Worth Statement

- On the following page, write a personal affirmation that reflects your intrinsic worth. Begin with "I am..." and focus on qualities and strengths that make you uniquely valuable.
  - Example: "I am strong, capable, and deserving of success. My journey is valid, and my story matters."

4. Turn Comparison into Inspiration

- Reflect on a time when you compared yourself to someone else and felt inadequate.
- Write down what you admired about that person and how you can apply those qualities to your own growth, without diminishing your unique journey.
  - Example: "I admired their confidence in public speaking. I can take a small step by volunteering to present in a supportive setting."

5. Set a Progress Goal

- Choose one area of your life where you feel pressure to be perfect (e.g., career, relationships, health).
- Write down one small, attainable goal to make progress in that area without focusing on perfection.
  - Example: Instead of saying, "I must write the perfect report," set the goal to "I will complete a first draft and revise, as needed."

REFLECTION QUESTIONS

- How has replacing negative labels with truths changed your perspective on your self-worth?
- What steps can you take to stop striving for perfection and instead celebrate progress?
- How does embracing your unique identity empower you to navigate challenges with confidence?

_____
_____
_____
_____
_____
_____
_____
_____
_____
_____
_____
_____
_____
_____
_____
_____
_____
_____
_____
_____
_____
_____
_____
_____
_____

THE HOODED
VICTORY LAP

T he journey to my doctoral degree may have seemed to strictly
be an academic pursuit to many looking from the outside—
but it wasn't. It was a deeply personal triumph that marked my
refusal to be defined by limitations. When I think about the "hood" I
grew up in and the academic hood I now wear, the contrast is profound.
My story is one of transformation—from the streets of inner-city
Chicago to a place among the 1% of Black individuals with a doctorate.
My journey is not just my own; it belongs to the community that raised
me, the family I represent, and the countless others who dare to believe
they, too, can overcome.

From my earliest days, I was surrounded by challenges that sought
to define and limit me—poverty, systemic oppression, being a first-
generation college student, and navigating life as a single mother. I faced
barriers that told me my dreams were too big, my voice too insignificant,
and my existence unworthy of recognition. But I chose a different path.
I chose to break the cycles of generational curses and systemic injustice. I
chose to become a trailblazer, carving a path not only for myself, but for
others to follow.

The Decision to Keep Going

Earning a doctoral degree is a rigorous test of endurance, resilience, and self-belief. Early in my journey, my mentor's words echoed a truth I would carry through every twist and turn: "Every time you want to give up, you'll need to make the conscious decision to keep going" (Dr. Joy Coates). This was a roadmap for survival in a process that felt overwhelming and, at times, impossible.

The challenges were relentless. Balancing the demands of single parenthood with the pressures of academia left me stretched thin. Add to that the layers of systemic barriers, microaggressions, and the emotional toll of navigating spaces where I was often made to feel like I didn't belong. As a Black woman in academia, I faced biases that sought to erode my confidence. Gaslighting disguised as "constructive criticism" and a lack of mentorship reminded me that the system wasn't built with me in mind.

But what the system underestimated was my resolve. I had already faced challenges that prepared me for this moment—growing up in the inner city, navigating fatherlessness, and breaking generational cycles of limitation. I was not unfamiliar with uphill battles. The doubt cast upon me wasn't a reflection of my capabilities; it was a reflection of the world's inability to recognize the strength and determination within me.

Every time I questioned whether I had what it took, I anchored myself in the truth: I wasn't just pursuing a degree; I was walking in my calling. This journey was about breaking barriers, setting a precedent, and demonstrating that people like me could not only survive, but thrive in spaces that often sought to exclude us.

The moment I learned my chair had dropped me, just weeks before graduation, was one of the most trying moments of my academic journey. It felt like a targeted, retaliatory blow, aimed to undermine my progress. I was left with a choice: to succumb to defeat or to rise above the injustice. I chose the latter.

Finding a new chair so close to the finish line was no small feat. It meant restarting significant parts of my dissertation process, reworking what was already complete, and extending my timeline an additional year. Yet, I refused to let this setback define the end of my story. This was challenging, but my new chair Dr. Gyant, my mentor Dr. Coates, and cohort friend Dr. Silverman helped me through the abandonment and disappointment to attain completion. I poured every ounce of determination into finishing what I started. I leaned on my faith, sought guidance, and committed myself to the journey anew.

THE HOODED MOMENT

The following year, I graduated with my doctorate officially. When the moment finally arrived to receive my academic regalia and hood, it felt like the culmination of every trial, every late night, and every moment I doubted myself. That moment was a reclamation of power, a declaration that no obstacle, no systemic barrier, no act of retaliation could stop what was divinely purposed for me. What others intended to break me only fortified my spirit. My victory was personal.

Through this process, I learned that perseverance is not just about enduring challenges, but about actively choosing to rise above them. Each recommitment to the process, each decision to press forward in the face of adversity, became a brick in the foundation of my success. It reinforced a truth I now carry with me: resilience is built one decision at a time.

This journey proved to myself, my family, and my community that no dream is too big and no barrier insurmountable. My doctorate degree is a symbol of grit, a testimony of faith, and a ray of hope for anyone daring to believe in their own potential. It is a reminder to everyone facing seemingly insurmountable odds that success is possible when you refuse to give up. It is a legacy of perseverance, the ability to overcome, a call to action for others to persist, and proof that the decision to keep going is always worth it.

The hood I wore was about breaking barriers that were never meant to be broken, about shattering glass ceilings and redefining what was possible for someone like me. It was about the girl from the hood of Chicago who dared to dream beyond her circumstances and the woman who turned those dreams into reality. That hood represented my family, my community, and every single person who had ever been told they weren't enough.

A Symbol of Legacy

Standing on that stage as Dr. Shatoya Black was a full-circle moment. It was a transition from the hood I grew up in to the hood I wore—a powerful visual representation of triumph over adversity. The name "Dr. Shatoya Black" carried a weight far greater than the letters that preceded it. It demanded respect, not because of the title alone, but because of the journey it represented.

For those who once doubted me, who dismissed my potential or underestimated my determination, the sight of me in that hood was undeniable. It was a visual proclamation that I had risen above the odds. The people who had dismissed my capabilities had no choice, but to acknowledge the grit, resilience, and determination that had propelled me to this point.

My hood carried the weight of a lifetime of perseverance. It was a victory lap—a declaration to the world and to myself that I had not only survived, but thrived. It was a visible symbol of my journey, a journey marked by struggle, pain, hardship, abandonment, rejection, and faith. My hood symbolized the battles I fought—against stereotypes, against systemic oppression, and even against my own insecurities. It stood as proof to the fact that where you come from doesn't define where you're going.

The hood wasn't just for me—it was for everyone who had walked with me through this journey. It was for my family, who sacrificed and supported me in ways I could never repay. It was for my community, who often felt the weight of systemic barriers, but continued to persevere. It was for every young person who saw in me a reflection of their own potential.

In that moment, I wasn't just celebrating my victory—I was celebrating the triumph of a collective. I carried my community on my shoulders, and the weight of their dreams only made me stand taller. That hood became a symbol of what's possible when faith, resilience, and determination intersect.

As I stood there, I felt the gravity of what it meant to be Dr. Shatoya Black. It was a name that honored not only my journey, but also the countless others who had walked similar paths and those who would come after me. My hooded moment was a new beginning, one that invited others to step boldly into their own journeys of transformation and triumph.

Impacting Family, Community, and Beyond

This victory wasn't just mine—it belonged to my family, my community, and the generations that came before me. My achievement was a culmination of sacrifices, prayers, and perseverance that extended far beyond my own efforts. It became a shared triumph, one that rippled through the lives of those who had supported, inspired, and believed in me along the way.

For my family, this moment was monumental. It was proof that barriers could be broken and cycles could be transformed. My daughter, especially, witnessed firsthand what it meant to dream boldly, work relentlessly, and overcome the odds. She saw that success wasn't just about individual accomplishments, but about creating pathways to success for others to follow. My journey became a roadmap for her own aspirations, a reminder that she, too, could rise above challenges and make a lasting impact.

In my community, my achievement was celebrated as a collective win. People saw in my story a reflection of their own potential and the possibilities that existed beyond their circumstances. It wasn't just about me earning a degree—it was about proving that someone from the same streets, the same struggles, could rise above and achieve greatness. My victory became a symbol of hope, a message that no dream was too big and no obstacle was too great to overcome.

My journey didn't just inspire admiration; it inspired action. It encouraged others to believe in their worth, to reject the limits imposed upon them, and to take bold steps toward their goals. Whether it was a young student doubting their abilities, a single parent balancing life's demands, or a community seeking change, my story resonated deeply. It reminded them that success wasn't reserved for the privileged few—it was attainable for anyone willing to persevere.

In that moment, I realized that my victory was a legacy in the making. It was a movement about empowering others to step into their own potential. The impact stretched far beyond the ceremony, influencing lives, igniting dreams, and laying the foundation for a brighter future. This life declared loudly and proudly: no matter where you start — the possibilities are limitless.

Celebrating the Journey

As I look back to reflect on my journey, I'm reminded of the challenges that could have stopped me—but didn't. Every sleepless night spent balancing responsibilities, every tear shed in moments of exhaustion or frustration, and every flicker of self-doubt that I had overcome served as proof of my purpose. The hard times weren't merely obstacles—they were the foundation of my transformation. They taught me perseverance, fortified my faith, and revealed strengths I didn't know I had.

I celebrated not just the degree, but the person I had become in the process. The journey had reshaped me into someone stronger, more determined, and more grounded in purpose. It wasn't just about the title of "Dr." before my name—it was about what it represented. It was about breaking barriers, defying odds, and standing as living proof to the power of faith, hard work, and unrelenting determination.

This was a celebration. I celebrated everything that aided in carrying me through the darkest moments, but above all, I celebrated God's unwavering faithfulness and grace. Every step of the journey bore His fingerprints, from the opportunities that opened doors to the moments when His strength was made perfect in my weakness. I knew I hadn't walked this path alone; His guidance had been the light that led me through every trial and every triumph. He sent genuine people– every step of the way– to become my village.

This was a journey of becoming—of growing into the fullness of who God had created me to be. I honored the struggles that shaped me, the lessons that taught me, and the victories that affirmed me. The journey was about stepping into a greater purpose, one that went beyond personal success to impact others and glorify God.

This victory reminded me to embrace every facet of who I am—a pioneer, strategist, solutionist, agent of C.H.A.N.G.E.™, creator of Unique I.M.P.A.C.T.™, advocate, influencer, and a voice of inspiration and empowerment. I celebrated the faithfulness of God, who had carried me through every season and brought me to this place of triumph. From hood to hooded is my victory lap and a celebration of the journey that has made me who I am.

* * *

STRATEGY OF SUCCESS: CELEBRATING YOUR JOURNEY

This activity encourages you to reflect on your personal journey, recognize the significance of your victories, and honor the growth that came from your challenges. By celebrating your successes—both big and small—you will acknowledge your resilience and inspire yourself to continue striving toward your purpose.

1. Reflect on Your Journey

- Create a timeline of your journey. Start with a challenge or significant obstacle you've faced and mark key moments of growth, breakthroughs, and victories along the way.
  - Example:
    - "I overcame self-doubt and enrolled in school."
    - "I completed a project despite limited resources."
    - "I graduated despite numerous setbacks."
    - Take time to appreciate how each moment shaped you and contributed to your growth.

2. Define Your Victory Lap

- Write down a major victory or accomplishment you've achieved (e.g., finishing school, starting a business, or reaching a personal milestone).
- Reflect on the following questions:
  - What challenges did you overcome to achieve this?
  - How did this accomplishment impact your life and those around you?
  - What lessons did you learn along the way?

_____

_____

_____

_____

_____

_____

_____

3. Celebrate Small Wins

- List five "small wins" you've experienced recently. These might be moments that seemed insignificant at the time, but contributed to your overall progress.
  - Example:
    - "I stuck to my schedule for a week."
    - "I asked for help when I needed it."
    - Reflect on how these small wins are building toward your larger goals.

_____

_____

_____

_____

_____

_____

_____

4. Create a Victory Affirmation

- Write a personal affirmation to celebrate your journey and remind yourself of your resilience.
  - Example: "I am proud of how far I've come. My journey is unique, and every step—both the struggles and triumphs—has made me stronger."

5. Plan Your Next Victory Lap

- Choose one goal or aspiration you're currently working toward.
- Break it into smaller milestones and identify one actionable step you can take this week to move closer to achieving it.
  - Example: If your goal is to write a book, your milestone could be to outline the chapters, and your actionable step could be to draft the introduction

REFLECTION QUESTIONS

- How have the challenges in your journey shaped your character and resilience?
- What does it mean to celebrate your victories—not just the destination, but the process that brought you there?
- How can you use your story to inspire others who are walking a similar path?

_____

_____

_____

_____

_____

_____

_____

_____

_____

_____

_____

_____

_____

_____

_____

_____

_____

_____

_____

_____

_____

_____

_____

_____

_____

_____

_____

_____

_____

_____

_____

From Oppression to Opportunity

S ystemic oppression is not an abstract concept—it is a lived reality for countless individuals and communities. It operates through invisible mechanisms woven into the fabric of society, perpetuating inequities across generations. These mechanisms, from discriminatory policies to economic barriers, create roadblocks that quietly dictate access to education, housing, and upward mobility.

For years, I internalized the struggles I faced, believing they were solely the result of my own shortcomings. The world told me that I wasn't doing enough, that I wasn't smart enough, or that I simply needed to work harder. But as I gained education and awareness, I began to understand a deeper truth: many of the challenges I faced were engineered by systemic forces designed to hold people like me back. These systems weren't just hurdles—they were chains. Recognizing this truth was the first step toward breaking free.

Redlining: A Legacy of Exclusion

Redlining stands as one of the most glaring examples of systemic oppression, a practice deeply rooted in racial discrimination. It was a calculated method used to deny individuals and families access to housing, loans, and financial opportunities based solely on their race and the neighborhoods they lived in. The term "redlining" originates from the literal red lines drawn on maps by the federal government and banks to mark areas deemed "hazardous" or "undesirable" for investment— predominantly Black and immigrant neighborhoods. This systemic exclusion wasn't just about denying mortgages; it was about denying entire communities the chance to build wealth, stability, and opportunity.

Growing up in Chicago, a city long known for its racial segregation, I saw firsthand how redlining shaped the landscape of my community. The lingering effects were not just visible—they were palpable. Families that worked tirelessly, saved responsibly, and demonstrated financial discipline were still denied the ability to purchase homes, one of the most reliable pathways to generational wealth in America. The message was clear: no matter how hard you worked, your zip code and skin color were barriers that could not be overcome by effort alone.

The systematic denial of mortgages and loans left Black neighborhoods deprived of investment. Without the ability to buy homes, residents couldn't build equity, pass wealth to future generations, or access the stability that comes with homeownership. The impact extended beyond individual families. Entire neighborhoods were left to languish without investment, their streets riddled with neglect, their schools underfunded, and their businesses struggling to survive.

Although redlining was officially outlawed with the Fair Housing Act of 1968, its legacy persists. A 2020 study starkly revealed the continued racial disparities in lending practices. In Chicago, for every dollar loaned in predominantly white neighborhoods, only 12 cents were loaned in Black neighborhoods and 13 cents in Latino neighborhoods. These disparities highlight how redlining, though illegal, continues in practice through modern-day policies and prejudices.

The effects are cyclical. When banks refuse to invest in certain neighborhoods, property values stagnate or decline, tax revenues dwindle, and essential community services suffer. Schools, which are often funded by local property taxes, become chronically underfunded, perpetuating educational inequities that keep the cycle of poverty turning. Businesses are reluctant to move into areas labeled as high-risk, reducing job opportunities and stifling economic growth.

Understanding the history and impact of redlining brought clarity to the struggles I had witnessed in my neighborhood. It became apparent that the challenges my community faced were not due to a lack of effort, intelligence, or potential, but the deliberate effects of a system designed to hold us back. Redlining wasn't just an act of economic discrimination; it was an attack on identity and self-worth, sending the message that some people's lives were worth less than others.

Despite this grim history, I found empowerment in knowledge. Understanding the roots of systemic oppression allowed me to see through the lies I had been told about my community and myself. It gave me the language and tools to challenge these systems and to advocate for equitable policies.

The fight against redlining is far from over. While we may not see literal red lines on maps today, the invisible barriers they created continue to deny opportunities to entire communities. Addressing these disparities requires intentional investment in historically marginalized neighborhoods, equitable lending practices, and policies that uplift rather than exclude.

Most importantly, it demands that we challenge the narrative that blames individuals for systemic failures. The resilience and resourcefulness I witnessed in my community were not just reactions to oppression —they were proof of potential waiting to be unleashed. The people I grew up with were not the problem; the system was. Recognizing this truth is the first step toward dismantling it and creating a society where everyone has a fair chance to thrive.

EDUCATIONAL INEQUITIES

Education is often celebrated as the great equalizer—the ladder that allows anyone, regardless of their background, to climb to success. Yet for countless students, particularly those from low-income and marginalized communities, that ladder is broken before they even begin to climb. The disparities in educational funding, resources, and opportunities mean that for many, the playing field is anything, but level.

In the United States, schools are largely funded by local property taxes. This system inherently disadvantages schools in low-income neighborhoods, where property values are lower and tax revenues are insufficient to meet the needs of students. As a result, these schools are chronically underfunded compared to their wealthier counterparts. This inequitable distribution of resources translates to larger class sizes, outdated textbooks, insufficient technology, and limited access to advanced placement courses or extracurricular programs.

I experienced these inequities firsthand. While I had teachers who were passionate, skilled, and deeply invested in their students, their hands were often tied by a lack of resources. It wasn't uncommon to see teachers spending their own money to purchase basic classroom supplies, from paper and pencils to books and art materials. The schools I attended didn't have the latest technology, enrichment opportunities, or robust college-preparatory programs that wealthier districts could afford.

These disparities extended beyond academics. The extracurricular opportunities that help students discover their passions and develop leadership skills were often absent or underfunded. Music programs, art classes, sports teams, and STEM clubs—pillars of a well-rounded educa-tion—were luxuries we couldn't afford. This lack of access not only hindered academic achievement, but also limited students' exposure to experiences that could spark ambition and confidence.

For students in underfunded schools, the message is clear: the system doesn't value your potential. The psychological impact of this inequity cannot be understated. Growing up in such an environment, it's easy to internalize the belief that you're inherently behind or that your dreams are out of reach. This can erode confidence and self-worth, leaving many students feeling defeated before they even have a chance to begin.

THE SCHOOL-TO-PRISON PIPELINE

Perhaps the most damaging consequence of systemic oppression in education is the school-to-prison pipeline. This national trend funnels students, disproportionately Black and Brown, out of classrooms and into the criminal justice system. Zero-tolerance policies, harsh discipli-nary practices, and the criminalization of minor infractions create an environment where students are treated as offenders rather than learners.

I witnessed this pipeline in action where Black and Brown students were often disciplined more harshly than their White peers for the same behaviors. While a White student might receive a warning, counseling, or a second chance, a Black or Brown child engaging in similar behavior was far more likely to face suspension, expulsion, or even arrest. This disparity in disciplinary practices reinforced harmful stereotypes and perpetuated a cycle of inequality.

The consequences of the school-to-prison pipeline are devastating. Students who are pushed out of classrooms are more likely to drop out, face unemployment, and ultimately enter the criminal justice system. Harsh disciplinary practices don't just punish students—they derail their futures. A single suspension or expulsion can mark a child for life, setting them on a path that's difficult, if not impossible, to escape.

FIGHTING BACK

Understanding these systemic inequities was a turning point for me. I began to see the struggles I experienced—and the struggles my commu-nity faced—not as individual failings, but as the result of a deeply flawed system. This awareness fueled my determination to build beyond barri-ers, not as a victim, but as an advocate for change.

Breaking this cycle requires systemic reform. It demands a commit-ment to treating all children with fairness, dignity, and respect. Schools need to shift from punitive models of discipline to restorative practices that prioritize learning, growth, and accountability. Teachers and administrators must be trained to recognize and combat implicit biases that contribute to inequitable outcomes.

Equally important, we must address funding disparities. Schools in low-income communities need equitable funding to provide students with the resources and opportunities they deserve. This includes access to technology, updated materials, extracurricular activities, and college-preparatory programs.

Education should not be a privilege—it is a fundamental right. And while the road to equity is long, it begins with recognizing the problem, amplifying the voices of those affected, and committing to change.

Therefore, I urge you to educate yourself about the systemic barriers that exist in your community to become an advocate. Support policies and initiatives that aim to close access, opportunity, and funding gaps and eliminate discriminatory practices. Mentor a student, advocate for fairer discipline policies, or volunteer at a local school. Make the stance that you will not be the problem, but offer solutions.

Above all, remember this: every has potential. It is our responsibility to ensure that the systems in place nurture that potential rather than stifle it. By addressing educational inequities, we can transform not just individual lives, but entire communities, creating a legacy of opportunity and empowerment for generations to come.

THE PSYCHOLOGICAL TOLL OF OPPRESSION

The weight of systemic oppression goes far beyond external barriers—it seeps into the mind, influencing how we view ourselves, our worth, and our potential. It is a subtle, insidious force, constantly whispering that we are "less than," that our best efforts will never be good enough, and that success is meant for others, not for us. These messages and perspec-tives are not always explicit, but they are pervasive, reinforced by societal structures, biased systems, and even well-meaning individuals who fail to recognize the harm their words and actions perpetuate.

Over time, this narrative creates an exhausting cycle of self-doubt and frustration, making it feel as though escape is impossible. It can paralyze ambition, stifle hope, and erode confidence, leaving behind a sense of despair that is difficult to shake.

I have felt this weight in deep personal ways. It's the anger and helplessness that comes with seeing your hard work dismissed, your talents overlooked, and your contributions undervalued—not because they lack merit, but because of systemic biases tied to who you are and where you come from. It's the heartbreak of watching others receive opportunities effortlessly while you fight for every inch of progress. It's the sinking realization that no matter how many hours you work, how many degrees you earn, or how much you pour into your goals, the system wasn't built to reward your efforts.

For me, this toll often manifested as exhaustion—not just physical, but emotional and spiritual. It's the kind of fatigue that comes from constantly navigating spaces that were never designed for your presence, where your achievements are minimized, and where your very existence can feel like a challenge to the status quo.

The psychological impact of oppression is not abstract; it reveals itself in tangible, often debilitating ways. Chronic anxiety becomes a constant companion, fueled by the uncertainty of whether your efforts will ever be enough. Depression takes root as hope dwindles, and the belief that change is possible feels more like a distant dream than an achievable reality.

Even physical health begins to suffer. The unrelenting stress of navigating systemic inequities can lead to elevated cortisol levels, which wreak havoc on the body. Sleep becomes elusive, and the ability to focus or make decisions becomes clouded by the weight of it all. These symptoms are not just individual struggles—they are the product of a system that thrives on keeping people marginalized, exhausted, and disconnected.

The isolation that comes with oppression further compounds its effects. When the narrative of "not enough" is repeated often enough, it becomes easy to internalize. You begin to question your abilities, your worth, and your place in the world. The blame shifts inward, convincing you that the fault lies not in the system, but within yourself. This is one of the greatest tragedies of systemic oppression: its ability to make people believe they are the problem rather than recognizing the structures designed to keep them down.

Becoming a Cycle Breaker

Recognizing the psychological toll of oppression is an essential first step toward healing and liberation. For me, this acknowledgment was a turning point. It allowed me to name the feelings of inadequacy, frustra-tion, and hopelessness for what they were—not a reflection of my value or effort, but the intended outcome of a system built to exclude and devalue people like me.

This realization brought with it a sense of empowerment. By understanding the root cause of my struggles, I could begin to dismantle the lies I had internalized. The belief that I wasn't enough was not born out of truth, but out of systemic efforts to suppress my potential. With this awareness, I could reject the narrative and start to rewrite my story.

Understanding the psychological impact of oppression is not about dwelling in pain, but about reclaiming power. It's about recognizing that the weight you feel is not yours alone to bear. It's about rejecting the lie that you are the problem and embracing the truth that you are more than enough.

Through this process, I have learned to see my challenges not as overwhelming obstacles, but as opportunities for growth and advocacy. The very systems that sought to break me became the catalyst for my purpose. By naming and addressing the psychological toll of oppression, I have been able to turn my pain into power, using my story to inspire and empower others.

To anyone carrying the weight of oppression as a cycle breaker, I want you to know this: the problem is not you. Your worth is not defined by the structures around you or the lies you've been told. You have the power to break free, to reclaim your identity, and to rewrite your story. You are enough, and your journey matters. Let the weight you've carried become the foundation for the legacy you are building.

From Awareness to Empowerment

Education became the lens through which I could finally see the intri-cate structures of systemic oppression. It illuminated the barriers I once thought were personal failings, revealing them as deliberate systems designed to suppress. This clarity was empowering—not because it excused the challenges I faced, but because it equipped me to approach those challenges with a shift in mindset geared toward solutions.

Through education, I gained the vocabulary and tools to identify these systemic barriers for what they were: obstacles, not immovable walls. Rather than allowing hopelessness to consume me, I began to strategize. What could I do to rebuilt? How could I make a difference—not just for myself, but for others walking similar paths?

Awareness alone, however, wasn't enough. *Knowledge without action is powerless.* I understood that to create real change, I had to step into a position of advocacy. Armed with the knowledge I had gained, I began to innovatively build, creating strategies that aligned us to challenge inequitable systems, demand accountability, and amplify the voices of those who had been silenced. I became an advocate pushing for policies and practices that closed the opportunity and access gap, instead of perpetuating oppression.

The journey to breaking free from systemic oppression requires a shift in perspective. It's easy to see yourself as a victim of your circumstances, weighed down by a system that seems impenetrable. But as your awareness grows, you will realize that you are not powerless. Personally, I realized that I could become an agent of C.H.A.N.G.E.™—a force capable of shaping the world around me.

This transformation was anything, but easy. It required resilience, faith, and a relentless commitment to personal growth. I had to confront internalized narratives that told me I wasn't enough, dismantling the lies that had taken root over years of societal conditioning.

Equipping myself with knowledge became one of my most powerful weapons. I sought out mentors who could guide me and pursued education as a means of empowerment. I immersed myself in communities of people who believed in my potential, who reminded me that my value was inherent, not contingent on external validation.

Above all, my faith anchored me. It reminded me that my worth was not dictated by man-made systems, but by the God who had designed me with a unique purpose. That faith gave me the courage to stand firm in the face of adversity, being ostracized, misunderstood, but knowing that I was equipped with everything I needed to overcome.

My journey from oppression to opportunity was never meant to be a solo endeavor. I understood that my transformation could become a catalyst for the transformation of others. Each barrier I broke was a pathway to success that I cleared for someone else to walk through.

Through community-building, advocacy, and mentorship, I dedicated myself to rewriting the narrative of how individuals targeted by oppressive systems were perceived. Whether through mentoring young people, advocating for equitable education policies, creating spaces for underrepresented voices to be heard, designing innovative experiences, or providing language that empowers, I committed to building a legacy of transformation and empowerment.

This work is not without its challenges. Systemic oppression is deeply ingrained, and progress often feels incremental. But every small victory, every life impacted, is a reminder of why the fight is worth it. The effects of this work extend far beyond what I can see in the present, reaching into future generations and creating possibilities I may never witness.

TOGETHER, WE CREATE OPPORTUNITY

The journey from oppression to opportunity is a collective responsibility. When we choose to educate ourselves, to advocate for equity, and to amplify the voices of the marginalized, we create a world where everyone has the chance to thrive.

This is our call to action. Let us rise to it with courage, compassion, and determination. The time for change is now, and it starts with each of us doing our part to build a future where oppression is dismantled and opportunity is abundant.

1. **Educate Yourself**: Understanding is the first step to dealing with oppression. Learn about the systems at play—how they operate and whom they affect. Read, listen, and engage with the stories of those who have lived under these structures. Knowledge is the foundation of meaningful action.

2. **Advocate for Change**: Whether in education, housing, criminal justice, or other systems, use your voice to support policies and initiatives that promote equity. Write to your representatives, vote with intention, and join movements that work toward systemic reform.

3. **Elevate Our Collective Voices**: Those most affected by systemic oppression often have the clearest insights into its effects and solutions. Amplify their voices. Create platforms for their stories to be heard. Their perspectives are essential in shaping meaningful change.

Together, we can turn the tide—one step, one voice, one act of faith at a time. Change begins with each of us— through awareness and consistent action.

* * *

STRATEGY OF SUCCESS: BARRIERS TO BRIDGES

This activity empowers you to identify systemic barriers you've faced, reflect on how they've influenced your life, and develop strategies to turn those obstacles into opportunities. By focusing on solutions and leveraging your knowledge and resilience, you can take steps to overcome oppression and create meaningful change.

1. Identify the Systemic Barriers

- Reflect on areas in your life where you've experienced systemic barriers (e.g., education, employment, access to resources).
- Write down specific examples of how these barriers have impacted you or your community.
  - Example: "Limited access to quality education meant fewer opportunities to explore my interests in school."

2. Reframe the Narrative

- For each barrier you listed, write down how facing this challenge has shaped your perspective or strengthened your resilience.
  - Example: "Limited resources taught me to be resourceful and seek out creative solutions."
- Reframing doesn't dismiss the injustice—it highlights your strength and ability to adapt despite it.

_____

_____

_____

_____

_____

_____

3. Develop an Action Plan

- Identify one systemic barrier you identified and brainstorm ways to address or overcome it.
- Write down a step you can take to work toward a solution, whether it's personal (e.g., pursuing education) or communal (e.g., advocating for policy changes).
  - Example:
    - Barrier: Lack of access to affordable housing
    - Action: Attend a community meeting on housing advocacy or volunteer with an organization addressing this issue.

_____

_____

_____

_____

_____

_____

4. Create a Personal Empowerment Statement

- Write a statement that affirms your power to overcome and turn systemic barriers into opportunities.
- Example: "I am not defined by the systemic barriers I've faced. I have the strength, knowledge, and faith to transform challenges into opportunities for growth and change."

5. Engage in Advocacy or Community Building

- Identify a way you can contribute to creating systemic change in your community. Write it in the box below.
  - Examples:
    - Join a local advocacy group.
    - Mentor someone navigating similar challenges.
    - Share your story to inspire others.

Reflection Questions

- How has awareness of systemic barriers helped you approach challenges with a solution-oriented mindset?
- What steps can you take to transform oppression into opportunity, both in your life and in your community?
- How can you leverage your unique voice and experiences to create meaningful change?

_____
_____
_____
_____
_____
_____
_____
_____
_____
_____
_____
_____
_____
_____
_____
_____
_____
_____
_____
_____
_____
_____
_____
_____

VOICES OF TRIUMPH

Every voice carries its own unique power, shaped by the paths we walk, the battles we fight, and the obstacles we overcome. For too long, however, the voices born from lived experiences—especially those forged in systemic oppression, poverty, and social marginalization—have been undervalued and dismissed. These voices are reservoirs of wisdom, strength, knowledge, and truth that can't be captured by theories or confined to academic frameworks. They hold perspectives that transcend classroom learning, offering insights that only life itself can teach.

Yet, in a society that often prioritizes credentials over compassion and titles over truth, these voices are silenced. Instead of being welcomed and amplified, they are diminished, cast aside as less credible because they don't fit the traditional molds of authority.

I know this dismissal all too well. As a nontraditional and first-generation student returning to higher education after years of community work, I carried with me a wealth of real-world knowledge. I had witnessed, firsthand, the impact of poverty, systemic barriers, and societal inequities. When I entered the classroom, I thought this experience would be an asset—a lens through which I could contribute to the conversation.

One day, in a class discussing ecological systems theory—a framework designed to examine how individuals interact with their environments—I saw an opportunity to speak up. The professor was teaching with a sterile detachment, presenting the realities of poverty as abstract concepts, devoid of human connection. I raised my hand, eager to add context from my lived experience. I believed I could provide a perspective that no textbook could encapsulate, one rooted in truth, resilience, and survival. *But I was silenced.*

The professor dismissed me, saying my opinion didn't matter because I didn't have the credentials to back it up. I hadn't published papers or earned degrees, so my lived experience—my *firsthand* expertise—was deemed irrelevant. Meanwhile, my peers, most of whom had never lived the realities we were discussing, were free to contribute their perspectives without question.

At that moment, I felt the sting of systemic devaluation. My voice, shaped by years of surviving and thriving in the very conditions they studied, was ignored because it didn't fit their predefined idea of "expertise."

The Disconnect Between Experience & Expertise

This dismissal of lived experience is not unique to me; it reflects a broader societal issue. In many spaces, traditional measures of expertise—degrees, titles, institutional affiliations—are treated as the ultimate authority. While these credentials have their place, they often come at the expense of equally valuable lived experiences.

Society tends to overlook that lived experience is its own form of expertise. It fosters resilience, adaptability, and resourcefulness. It equips individuals with insights that can't be found in a classroom or on a resume. Yet, in educational and professional settings, cultural and social capital—the skills, knowledge, and networks developed through life's challenges—are frequently undervalued.

This disconnect isn't just a personal injustice; it's a systemic failure. By silencing voices shaped by real-world adversity, we lose critical perspectives that could drive transformative change. We perpetuate cycles of exclusion and dehumanization, valuing theory over reality and credentials over compassion.

The irony is that these lived experiences often serve as the very foundation of resilience. Those who endure systemic barriers develop a level of resourcefulness, creativity, and tenacity that traditional systems of authority cannot replicate. When these qualities are dismissed, it's not just an individual loss—it's a societal one. We miss out on innovative solutions, new ways of thinking, and perspectives that could address systemic problems more effectively than theoretical approaches ever could.

By failing to acknowledge lived experiences as valid and valuable, we reinforce a hierarchy of knowledge that excludes the very voices that could lead us toward equity and justice.

THE PSYCHOLOGICAL TOLL OF DEVALUATION

Being told that your voice doesn't matter and that your experience is irrelevant, can chip away at your sense of self. For me, being silenced in that classroom made me question my place in higher education. It made me feel invisible, as though my life's journey—the challenges I had over-come, the wisdom I had gained—held no value.

This type of dismissal can foster feelings of inadequacy and self-doubt, leaving you to wonder if you belong anywhere at all. When you're constantly told, directly or indirectly, that you are "less than," it becomes easy to internalize that narrative. You may begin to question your perspective and whether your efforts to succeed are futile in a system that wasn't designed for you.

The psychological toll doesn't stop there. It can seep into your aspirations, limiting how far you believe you can go. The systemic barriers that silence your voice may also magnify feelings of isolation, frustration, and despair. The result is a toxic cycle that can leave marginalized individuals struggling to prove their value in spaces that refuse to recognize it.

I've felt that weight—the exhaustion of trying to navigate a world that devalues you at every turn, the anger of knowing you have something to contribute, but aren't allowed to share it, and the despair of wondering if things will ever change. But through time and reflection, I realized something powerful: the issue wasn't my voice—it was the system that tried to suppress it.

Reclaiming the Power of Lived Experiences

That realization was liberating. I began to see my lived experiences not as liabilities, but as assets. I learned to reject the false narratives imposed on me and to embrace the truth of my journey. My voice, forged in the fire of adversity, held a power that no title or credential could replicate.

I also began to recognize the broader value of lived experiences—not just my own, but those of the people around me. Communities that have faced systemic oppression are reservoirs of strength, creativity, and resilience. Their stories hold the keys to understanding and dismantling the very systems that seek to silence them.

Reclaiming the power of lived experiences isn't just about speaking up; it's about transforming those experiences into tools for empowerment. It's about creating spaces where marginalized voices can be heard, valued, and amplified. It's about challenging the systems that dehumanize and exclude, and advocating for policies and practices that celebrate the richness of diverse perspectives.

One of the most profound ways to honor lived experiences is by creating spaces where people feel safe to share their truths. Trusted spaces—whether in classrooms, workplaces, or communities—are environments where individuals can speak without fear of judgment or rejection.

For those who have been silenced, trusted spaces can be deeply impactful and transformative, as they can allow for healing, connection, and empowerment. They can also give individuals the courage to step into their voices and share their stories, knowing that they will be met with respect and understanding.

Building these spaces requires intentionality. It means listening with empathy, valuing authenticity over conformity, and dismantling the unspoken norms that perpetuate exclusion. For educators, leaders, and organizations, it means actively seeking out and amplifying the voices of those who have been marginalized.

We must move beyond tokenism and performative gestures to truly elevate lived experiences. This means listening, validating, and integrating these voices into decision-making processes. It means acknowledging the systemic barriers that have historically silenced them and working actively to dismantle those barriers.

For me, the journey from being dismissed to becoming Dr. Shatoya Black was a testament to the power of lived experiences. I turned my struggles into strengths, my pain into purpose, and my silence into a voice that amplifies others.

It took time, reflection, and resilience, but I came to understand that my voice mattered—not despite my lived experience, but because of it. My journey from the hood to hooded, from silenced to amplified, has been one of liberation. I realized that the very thing dismissed as irrelevant was my greatest asset.

Your voice is a tool for liberation—not only for yourself, but for those who have yet to find theirs. By sharing your story authentically and confidently, you challenge the status quo. You become a catalyst for change, showing others that their lived experiences are valid, valuable, and powerful.

Empowerment Through Sharing

Empowering others begins with empowering yourself. It's the recognition that your voice matters. Sharing your truth is not only an act of self-affirmation, but also a catalyst for change in your community and beyond. It is a bold declaration that your experiences, insights, and perspectives are valuable and deserving of attention. Here's how you can step into this empowerment and, in doing so, inspire and uplift others.

1. Recognize the Value of Your Voice

Your lived experiences are your unique expertise. They carry insights that no degree or title can replicate. The struggles you've faced, the lessons you've learned, and the resilience you've developed are invaluable tools for navigating the world. It's easy to undervalue your voice in systems that prioritize traditional credentials or theoretical knowledge, but lived experience offers a depth of understanding that cannot be taught in a classroom.

Start by embracing the truth that your voice has power. Reflect on your journey and the knowledge you've gained through overcoming adversity. When you recognize the value of your voice, you give yourself permission to take up space and contribute meaningfully to conversations, no matter the setting.

2. Speak with Confidence

Reclaiming your narrative begins with speaking it boldly. Sharing your story is an act of courage and resistance against the systems and people that have sought to silence you. It's not about having all the answers or being perfect—it's about being authentic. Your vulnerability in sharing the highs and lows of your journey can inspire others, creating a domino effect of empowerment.

Confidence doesn't come overnight, but it grows with practice. Start by sharing your truth in trusted spaces, among people who uplift and support you. As you become more comfortable, expand your reach. Whether it's through public speaking, writing, or community forums, let your voice be heard. Remember, your story has the power to educate, inspire, and advocate for change.

3. Advocate for Others

Empowerment is about using your voice to amplify others. Advocacy involves recognizing the barriers that silence marginalized voices and actively working to dismantle them. When you've walked the path of finding your voice, you are uniquely positioned to guide others on their journey.

Advocacy can take many forms. It might mean mentoring someone who shares a similar background, speaking up for equitable policies, or sharing opportunities with those who have historically been excluded. Advocacy is about creating space for others to thrive, ensuring that their voices are heard, and using your platform to highlight the value of their experiences.

4. Build Inclusive Spaces

True empowerment happens in environments where people feel seen, heard, and valued. As you work to amplify your own voice, commit to building spaces where others can do the same. Whether in classrooms, workplaces, or community settings, strive to foster environments that celebrate diversity, encourage open dialogue, and prioritize inclusivity.

Building inclusive spaces requires intentionality. It involves challenging unspoken norms, addressing microaggressions, and ensuring that policies and practices promote equity. It's about creating a culture where everyone feels safe to share their truth without fear of judgment or rejection. As a leader, educator, or community member, your efforts to build these spaces can have a transformative impact.

A Legacy of Triumph

As we conclude this journey, I leave you with this truth: *your voice is your greatest asset.* It carries the power to challenge injustice, speak truth, and inspire change that extends far beyond what you can see. Your story, shaped by your lived experiences, holds a unique strength that no title or credential can replicate. Together, we can build a world where those experiences are not just acknowledged, but celebrated as vital contributions to our collective growth.

Your story is still unfolding, and your impact is limitless. Speak boldly, live authentically, and remember this: *you are the exception to the rule.* Let your voice lead the way—not just for yourself, but for those who come after you.

- **Honor the power of your lived experiences.** They are your truths, forged through resilience, struggle, perseverance, and triumph. Recognize their value and embrace them as part of your expertise. Speak up, even when it feels uncomfortable. Every time you share your story, you reclaim your narrative and affirm your worth.

- **Create space for others.** Empowerment is not just about lifting your own voice—it's about amplifying the voices of those who are still finding theirs. Advocate for systems and policies that elevate lived experiences. Listen to those whose voices have been silenced or overlooked, and challenge structures that perpetuate exclusion and injustice.

- **Build a future where every voice matters.** Work to create classrooms, workplaces, and communities where all voices are valued, and lived experiences are understood as critical tools for learning, empowerment, and transformation. Use your influence to dismantle barriers and replace them with opportunities for connection, growth, and equity.

Together, we can turn our voices into instruments of liberation. Together, we can create a world where stories like yours and mine are not only heard, but celebrated. Let your truth be your power. Let your story be your strength. And let your voice be the beacon that lights the way for others.

This is how we triumph— together.

STRATEGY OF SUCCESS: AMPLIFYING YOUR VOICE

This activity helps you discover the power of your voice, craft your story authentically, and build confidence in sharing it. By using your lived experiences as tools for empowerment, you can inspire and advocate for others while strengthening your own resolve.

1. Recognize Your Story's Value

- Reflect on a personal experience where your voice or story brought about change– whether in your life, someone else's, or your community.
- Write down the key lessons you learned from that experience
  - Example: "By sharing my struggles with education, I helped someone see that their circumstances don't define their potential."

2. Craft Your Narrative

- Using the experience you reflected on, outline a brief narrative with three parts:
  - Challenge: What obstacle or barrier did you face?
  - Turning Point: What action, realization, or support helped you overcome it?
  - Triumph: How did you grow, and what impact did it have on you or others?
  - Example:
    - Challenge: I felt silenced in academic settings.
    - Turning Point: I began to embrace my lived experiences as valid expertise.
    - Triumph: By sharing my voice, I inspired others to see value in their unique stories.

3. Practice Speaking Boldly

- Stand in front of a mirror or record yourself on your phone.
- Share your narrative confidently, focusing on clarity and authenticity.
- Repeat this practice regularly to build confidence in your storytelling ability.

4. Identify a Platform for Your Voice

- Think about where your story could make an impact. This could be:
  - A conversation with a friend or family member
  - A social media post or blog
  - A community event, support group, or advocacy space
- Take one tangible step to share your voice in that space.

5. Create Space for Others

- Reflect on how you can empower others to share their stories. Share your ideas in the box below.
- Consider starting a group, hosting a discussion, or simply being an active listener who affirms the value of others' experiences.

Reflection Questions

- How has sharing your story helped you reclaim your narrative?
- What impact has your voice had on others, and how can you expand that impact?
- How can you create environments where other voices are heard and valued?

_____
_____
_____
_____
_____
_____
_____
_____
_____
_____
_____
_____
_____
_____
_____
_____
_____
_____
_____
_____
_____
_____
_____
_____
_____

ACKNOWLEDGMENTS

> *"The first step to making an impact is being intentional in acknowledging what systemic oppressions and barriers are keeping the gaps of opportunity and access open. Once a pathway is created it is up to the person to follow."*
> – Dr. Shatoya Black

* * *

I acknowledge the decades of work by individuals who have spoken truth to power and provided resources, support, and services for under-represented communities. I hope we continue to build in ways that address the battle fatigue many experience while fighting against inequity. I also hope we become more aware of the silent victories we have won—victories that were never valued or even acknowledged, yet are a significant part of history often erased, even in the present.

We must remain mindful of holding people responsible and accountable for their actions, including those close to us, especially when others remain silent. The power of Unique I.M.P.A.C.T.™ lies in displaying love through action—self-advocacy for ourselves and empowerment for others—by elevating the voiceless and amplifying our own voices. I thank God in advance for the individuals who are making plans to change together, creating a unique impact and building a lasting legacy.

Legacy Life Navigators LLC extends its gratitude to all the partnerships, collaborations, organizations, businesses, and institutions that invited me to serve as a keynote speaker, facilitator for workshops, professional development trainer, and consultant to develop innovative initiatives. Thank you to everyone for your support and for taking the time to purchase and read our books.

About the Author

Dr. Shatoya Black is the CEO and Founder of Legacy Life Navigator LLC, which focuses on providing guidance and strategies for success. She is the past president of the Illinois TRIO Association, Project Director for Student Support Services (SSS) at Illinois State University, and a proud alumni of TRIO SSS at Northern Illinois University. Black was born and raised on the south side of Chicago and is the oldest of fourteen siblings. Her journey to college began without a place to call home, but she was offered a place to stay in DeKalb, Illinois, where she completed her degrees at Northern Illinois University, culminating in a doctorate in education.

She currently plays a strategically innovative role in developing initiatives that impact the holistic success of first-generation students and professionals, both personally and academically. With over fifteen years of experience, Dr. Black has dedicated her career to helping students navigate critical transition points in their lives.

Dr. Black has cultivated spaces that focus on closing the opportunity gap, building community, and addressing deficit perspectives and language to shift the narrative of first-generation students to an asset-based approach. She takes a holistic approach to success by highlighting the social and cultural capital students bring to the college environment. She has created intentional programming to elevate and amplify the voices of first-generation students' lived experiences.

Dr. Black has developed initiatives such as an inaugural campus-wide first-generation celebration, identity and career pathway development programs, student affinity groups, the First-Generation Triumph Podcast, direct-touch persistence, retention, and completion programs, First-Gen Fridays, financial enrichment programs, course development, innovative practical and experiential learning experiences, and language that liberates.

She has also implemented community impact projects that cultivate the 5A's of career development and has created a Legacy framework to guide students and professionals in identifying and navigating holistic success. Additionally, she founded the Unique I.M.P.A.C.T.™ initiative, which has been active for 15 years, and the C.H.A.N.G.E.™ initiative to inspire and empower others to embrace the change found within challenges.

Dr. Black draws on the impactful mentorship she received from TRIO association leaders during her own journey of growth and development to provide that same level of understanding and support to others as lifelong learners. She is an empowerment agent who believes that first-generation students and professionals face significant challenges in achieving their life goals without equitable opportunities. When there is a gap in opportunity, the ability to succeed often feels out of reach. Closing this gap requires identifying and addressing the factors keeping it open.

For more information or to get in contact with Shatoya, please scan the QR codes below.

Contact Dr. Black:

Dr. Black in the community:

www.ingramcontent.com/pod-product-compliance
Lightning Source LLC
Chambersburg PA
CBHW052118030426
42335CB00025B/3042